This book is dedicated to all of Meghann's cousins, Stephen, Liz, Peyton, and Andrew. The best cousins ever!!!

Thank you to your parents for leading by example. You taught your children to treat Meghann as a cousin first, then a cousin who happens to use a wheelchair. Cerebral Palsy did not define Meghann, and it definitely did not allow her to get away with anything around her family.

A special thank you to Gretchen Meyer for working with Meghann to give her a great beginning to live up to her full potential in life.

D1308261

"My name is Meghann. My friends call me

Meggeriffic!! I was born with Cerebral Palsy.

Cerebral Palsy means I have a weakness or

problems using my muscles. It affects

everyone differently."

"My cerebral palsy doesn't stop me from doing anything. How do I walk and move around?"

"Cuz, I can."

"This is me in my purple wheelchair."

"I use my wheelchair instead of my legs to get

around. I spin the wheels with my hands to

move in my wheelchair."

"This is Peyton. She is my cousin. I call her

Cuz."

"Peyton lives far away from me. I live in

Illinois, and she lives in Delaware. I like to

visit her."

"Can you find Illinois and Delaware on

the map?"

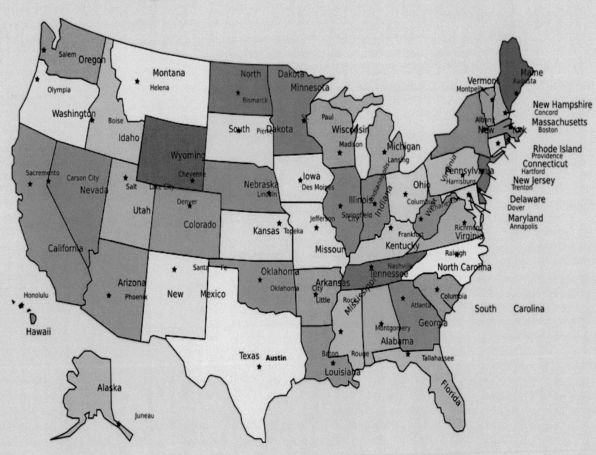

"Can you find where you live?"

"How do I go visit my cousin, Peyton?

Sometimes I fly in a plane to visit my cousin,

Peyton. Do you think I can fly in a plane?"

"Cuz, I can."

"This is an aisle wheelchair."

"When I get on the plane I get in this chair. It

is smaller than my wheelchair, and it gets me

to my seat on the plane."

"My wheelchair goes with all the suitcases on the plane. When I get to Delaware my wheelchair is waiting for me."

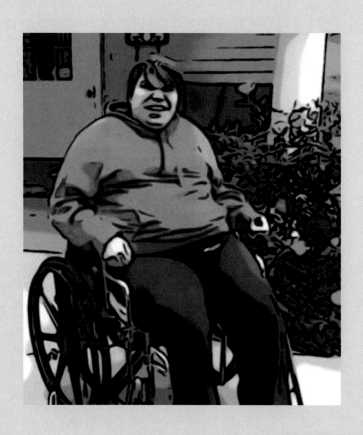

"This is a wheelchair."

"My Cuz, Peyton, and I have lots of fun together. We ride bikes, swim, kayak, go to the beach, and eat pizza."

KAYAK SWIM

BIKE

PIZZA

"Do you think I can ride a bike?"

"Cuz, I can."

"This is me on my bike when I was younger.

It's my mom's favorite picture. My bike is

bigger now."

"My bike has pulleys on the pedals. It makes it

easier for me to peddle. It also has a seat belt

to make sure I am safe. My cousin, Peyton, and

I bike all over with her friends."

"Sometimes my cousin, Peyton, and I like to go swimming. We go to the swimming pool in her town."

"Do you think I can get in the pool and

swim?"

"Cuz, I can."

"This is a pool lift chair. The chair lowers me

into the pool and lifts me out."

"Another fun thing Peyton and I like to do

is kayaking. Do you think I can go kayaking?"

"Cuz, I can."

"This is my Kayak. It has an extra piece to

keep me balanced."

"When I visit Peyton's house, we beg her mom

to take us to the beach. She always gives in."

Do you think I can go to the beach?"

"Cuz, I can."

"Some beaches have beach chairs for people

who can't use their legs like me. They have

giant wheels to get through the sand."

"When I am visiting my cousin, Peyton, we like to go out to eat pizza. Do you think I can go out to eat in my wheelchair?"

"Cuz, I can."

"Our favorite pizza place has a ramp that I can wheel up to get in. My cousin, Peyton uses the steps. Most of the time we race to see who gets to the door first."

"This is a ramp."

"What if the restaurant doesn't have a ramp?

Do you think I can still make it in the

restaurant?"

"Cuz, I can."

"This is a portable ramp. It folds up. I use it

when there is no ramp."

"After my visit with Peyton, her mom takes me

to the airport. I get back on a plane and fly

back to Illinois."

"Cuz, I can."

"Cerebral Palsy doesn't stop me from doing

anything. I might need to do it a little different,

and that's okay."

"Cuz, I can."

"I can travel, ride a bike, swim, kayak, go to

the beach, and go out for pizza. Maybe I will

parachute out of a plane."

"Cuz, I can."

"This is a parachute."

"Well...I think I will wait a while to jump out

of a plane."

"Cuz, I can. Right?"

"Cerebral Palsy or my wheelchair isn't going to stop me from doing anything that I love!!!

Someday I may become a teacher, doctor, therapist, or the President of the United States."

"Cuz, I can!!!"

The End

Seizures, wheelchairs, accessible equipment, obstacles, milestones, hospitals, advocating and questions were the words that consumed my life for over 30 years.

This is why I started a blog in 2015 to share my experiences and celebrate the small steps of accomplishments my daughter, Meghann, who was born with cerebral palsy achieved.

Meghann passed away on May 24, 2018 at 30 years old. Some of the words in my past have dropped out of my life but my passion to advocate has not stopped.

I hope this book will renew acceptance, teach, and inspire all people to strive to do whatever they wish in life. CUZ, THEY CAN.

If you would like to learn more about Meghann and our journey, follow the link below. You can also find the link to purchase or donate a copy of CUZ, I CAN.

https://parentingcelebratingsmallsteps.blogspot.com/

Feel free to contact me.   jillianm1963@hotmail.com